To Liz, as a lady - in - waiting
May 87

Much love
Corinne

GW00356848

Words of
JOY

Published by
Lion Publishing plc
Icknield Way, Tring, Herts, England
ISBN 0 85648 303 6
Albatross Books
PO Box 320, Sutherland, NSW 2232, Australia
ISBN 0 86760 212 0

First edition 1974, under the title *A Song of Joy*
Reprinted 1975, 1976, 1977, 1980, 1981,
1984 (twice), 1985

Photographs by Lion Publishing/David Alexander

Quotations from *Good News Bible*, copyright 1966,
1971 and 1976 American Bible Society; published
by Bible Societies/Collins

Printed and bound in Hong Kong

Words of
JOY

SING FOR JOY

Sing for joy to the Lord, all the world!
Worship the Lord gladly,
and come before him with joyful songs!

Never forget that the Lord is God!
He made us, and we belong to him;
we are his people, we are his flock.

Enter his temple with thanksgiving,
go into his sanctuary with praise!
Give thanks to him and praise him!

The Lord is good;
his love lasts for ever,
and his faithfulness for all time.

PSALM 100

A gateway into the ancient Temple area in the old city of Jerusalem.

YOU HAVE DONE GREAT THINGS

You answer us, God our Saviour,
and you save us by doing wonderful things.
People all over the world,
and across the distant seas, trust in you.

You set the mountains in place by your
strength,
showing your mighty power.
You calm the roar of the seas
and the noise of the waves;
you calm the uproar of the peoples.

The whole world is afraid,
because of the great things that you have
done.
Your actions bring shouts of joy
from one end of the earth to the other.

From PSALM 65

The sunlit waves of the Sea of Galilee, looking across
to the mountains on its western shore.

A NEW SONG

Sing a new song to the Lord!
Sing to the Lord, all the world!
Sing to the Lord, and praise him!
Every day tell the good news that he has
saved us!
Proclaim his glory to the nations,
his mighty acts to all peoples.

The Lord is great, and must be highly
praised;
he must be feared more than all the gods.
The gods of all other nations are only idols,
but the Lord made the heavens.
Glory and majesty are around him,
greatness and beauty are in his temple. . .

Be glad, earth and sky!
Roar, sea, and all the creatures in you;
be glad, fields, and everything in you!
Then the trees in the woods will shout for
joy before the Lord,
because he comes to rule the earth.
He will rule all peoples of the world
with justice and fairness.

From PSALM 96

Columbines growing on the slopes of Mount Gilboa.

JOY RESTORED

Create a pure heart in me, God,
and put a new and loyal spirit in me.
Do not banish me from your presence;
do not take your holy spirit away from me.
Give me again the joy that comes from your
salvation,
and make my spirit obedient.
Then I will teach sinners your commands,
and they will turn back to you.

Spare my life, God my Saviour,
and I will gladly proclaim your righteousness.
Help me to speak, Lord,
and I will praise you.

From PSALM 51

A lone donkey-rider takes a road by a stream.

GOD IS A GREAT KING

Clap your hands for joy, all peoples!
Praise God with loud songs!
The Lord, the Most High, is to be feared;
he is a great king, ruling over all the world.
He gave us victory over the peoples;
he made us rule over the nations.
He chose for us the land where we live,
the proud possession of his people,
whom he loves.

God goes up to his throne!
There are shouts of joy and the blast of
trumpets,
as the Lord goes up!
Sing praise to God;
sing praise to our king!
God is king over all the world;
praise him with songs!

From PSALM 47

A flight of stone steps at Ephesus, Turkey.

RULER OF ALL THINGS

Come, let us praise the Lord!
Let us sing for joy to our protector and
Saviour!
Let us come before him with thanksgiving,
and sing joyful songs of praise!

For the Lord is a mighty God,
a mighty king over all the gods.
He rules over the whole earth,
from the deepest caves to the highest hills.
He rules over the sea, which he made;
the land also, which he himself formed.

Come, let us bow down and worship him;
let us kneel before the Lord, our Maker!
He is our God;
we are the people he looks after,
the flock for which he provides.

From PSALM 95

The sun rises over the waters of the Dead Sea,
deeper below sea level than any other lake in the
world.

TRUE HAPPINESS

Listen to my words, Lord,
and hear my sighs.
My king and my God,
listen to my cry for help.

I will pray to you, Lord;
in the morning you hear my voice;
at sunrise I offer up my prayer,
and wait for your answer . . .

As for me, I can come into your house,
because of your great love;
I can worship in your holy temple,
and bow down to you in reverence. . .
Lord, I have many enemies;
lead me to do your will,
and make your way plain for me to follow!

All who find safety in you will rejoice;
they will always sing for joy.
You protect those who love you;
because of you they are truly happy.
You bless those who obey you, Lord;
your kindness protects them like a shield.

From PSALM 5

The light gleams on the ancient stones of a road
nearly 2,000 years old.

THE COURTS OF THE LORD

How I love your temple, Almighty God!
How I want to be there!
I long for the courts of the Lord's temple.
With my whole being I sing with joy to the
living God.

Even the sparrows have built a nest,
and the swallows have their own home;
they keep their young near your altars,
Lord Almighty, my king and my God.

How happy are those who live in your
temple,
always singing praise to you!

From PSALM 84

A natural temple is formed by the fronds of palms
near the River Jordan.

VICTORY FEAST

Praise the Lord!

Sing a new song to the Lord;
praise him in the meeting of his faithful
people!
Be glad, Israel, because of your creator;
rejoice, people of Zion, because of your king!
Praise his name with dancing;
play drums and harps in praise of him.

The Lord takes pleasure in his people;
he honours the humble with victory.
Let God's people rejoice in their triumph,
and sing joyfully at their feasts.

From PSALM 149

A desert-dweller offers hospitality in his tent.

RETURN FROM EXILE

When the Lord brought us back to Zion,
it was like a dream!
How we laughed, how we sang for joy!
Then the other nations said about us,
'The Lord did great things for them!'
Indeed he did great things for us;
how happy we were!

Lord, take us back to our land,
just as your rain brings water back to dry
riverbeds.
Let those who cried while they planted,
gather the harvest with joy!

Those who cried as they went out carrying
the seed
will come back singing for joy,
bringing in the harvest!

PSALM 126

An old man in the ancient town of Tsefat, Israel.

SADNESS INTO JOY

You have changed my sadness into a joyful
dance;
you have taken off my clothes of mourning,
and given me clothes of joy.
So I will not be silent;
I will sing praise to you.
Lord, you are my God,
I will give thanks to you for ever.

From PSALM 30

Brightly-coloured traditional cloths laid out for sale
in the market at Beersheba.

GOD IS NEAR

You, Lord, are all I have,
and you give me all I need;
my life is in your hands.
How wonderful are your gifts to me;
how good they are!

I praise the Lord, because he guides me,
and in the night my conscience warns me.
I am always aware of the Lord's presence;
he is near, and nothing can shake me.

And so I am full of happiness and joy,
and I always feel secure;
because you will not allow me to go to the
world of the dead,
you will not abandon to the depths below
the one you love.

You will show me the path that leads to life;
your presence fills me with joy,
and your help brings pleasure for ever.

From PSALM 16

The sun gleams on a lake in central Turkey while the
storm clouds gather.

JOY IN HARVEST

You show your care for the land by sending
rain;
you make it rich and fertile.
The streams you have given never run dry;
they provide the earth with crops—
this is what you have done.

You send abundant rain on the ploughed
fields
and soak them with water;
You soften the soil with showers
and cause the young plants to grow.

What a rich harvest your goodness provides!
Wherever you go there is plenty!
The pastures are filled with flocks;
the hillsides are full of joy.
The fields are covered with sheep;
the valleys are full of wheat;
they shout and sing for joy!

From PSALM 65

Donkeys pull a sled to thresh the corn in the hills of
Judea.

A LIGHT FOR MY PATH

How I love your law!
I think about it all day long.
Your commandment is with me all the time,
and makes me wiser than all my enemies. . .
How sweet is the taste of your rules;
they are sweeter than honey!
I gain wisdom from all your laws,
and so I hate bad conduct.

Your word is a lamp to guide me,
and a light for my path . . .
Your commandments are my eternal
possession;
they are the joy of my heart.

From PSALM 119

A pale sun gleams over the waters of the
Mediterranean.

GOD CARES

I will praise you, Lord, with all my heart,
I will tell all the wonderful things you have
done.
I will sing with joy because of you.
I will sing praise to you, Most High!

The Lord is a refuge for the oppressed,
a place of safety in times of trouble.
Those who know you, Lord, will trust you;
you do not abandon anyone who comes to
you.

Sing praise to the Lord, who rules in Zion!
Tell every nation what he has done!
God remembers those who suffer;
he does not forget their cry,
and he punishes those who wrong them.

From PSALM 9

A woman in the old city of Jerusalem, her load
carried on her head.

LET THE PEOPLE REJOICE

God, be merciful to us and bless us;
look on us with kindness,
that the whole world may know your will;
that all nations may know your salvation.

May the peoples praise you, God;
may all the peoples praise you!

May the nations be glad and sing for joy,
because you judge the peoples with justice
and guide all the nations.

May the peoples praise you, God;
May all the peoples praise you!

The land has produced its harvest;
God, our God, has blessed us.
God has blessed us;
may all people everywhere honour him.

PSALM 67

Two little girls enjoy a game in a narrow street of
old Jerusalem.

THE KING IS GLAD

The king is glad, Lord, because you gave
him strength;
he is full of joy, because you made him
victorious.
You have given him what he wanted;
you have answered his request.

You came to him with great blessings
and set a gold crown on his head.
He asked for life, and you gave it;
a long and lasting life.

His glory is great because of your help;
you have given him fame and majesty.
Your blessings are upon him for ever,
and your presence fills him with gladness.

From PSALM 21

The remains of the ancient splendours of Avdat,
city of the Negev desert, are silhouetted against the
setting sun.

JOY IN OLD AGE

You have taught me ever since I was young,
and I still tell of your wonderful acts . . .
Now that I am old and my hair is grey,
do not abandon me, God!
Be with me while I proclaim your power
and might
to all generations to come. . .

I will indeed praise you with the harp;
I will praise your faithfulness, my God.
On my harp I will play hymns to you,
the Holy One of Israel.
I will shout for joy as I play for you;
with my whole being I will sing,
because you have saved me.

From PSALM 71

Old age and youth in a town in central Turkey.

JOYFUL THANKS

How good it is to give thanks to the Lord,
to sing in your honour, Most High God,
to proclaim your constant love every
morning,
and your faithfulness every night,
with the music of stringed instruments,
and with melody on the harp.
Your mighty acts, Lord, make me glad;
because of what you have done I sing for joy.

From PSALM 92

A reconstruction of a frieze of Assyrian musicians,
from the time of the Psalms (from the Haifa Music
Museum).

SING FOR JOY

Sing for joy to the Lord, all the earth;
praise him with songs and shouts of joy!
Sing praises to the Lord with harps;
play music on the harps!
With trumpets and horns,
shout for joy before the Lord, the king!

Roar, sea, and all creatures in you;
sing, earth, and all who live there!
Clap your hands, oceans;
hills, sing together with joy before the Lord,
because he comes to rule the earth!
He will rule all peoples of the world
with justice and fairness.

From PSALM 98

Beyond the breakers the long hump of Mount
Carmel juts out into the sea.